Behind the Curtain: The Life and Legacy of Alan Rickman

Scotty N. Moore

All rights reserved. No part of this publication may be reproduced, distributed, or transmitted in any form or by any means, including photocopying, recording, or other electronic or mechanical methods, without the prior written permission of the publisher, except in the case of brief quotations embodied in critical reviews and certain other noncommercial uses permitted by copyright law.

Copyright © Scotty N. Moore, 2023.

Table Of Contents

Foreword:
Preface:
Introduction
- Overview of Alan Rickman's Life and Career
- Importance Of His Contributions To Cinema, Theater, And Culture

Chapter 1: Early Life and Education
- Family background and upbringing
- Education And Early Interests In Acting

Chapter 2: Starting Out in Theater
- Early theatrical activity in London and beyond

Chapter 3: Breakthrough Film Role

- [Landing the part of Hans Gruber in Die Hard](#)
- [Impact of the Performance and Subsequent Hollywood Success](#)

[Chapter 4: Versatile Career on Stage and Screen](#)
- [Varied Roles In Theater And Cinema](#)
- [Critical Praise For Performances In Many Genres And Forms](#)

[Chapter 5: Behind the Scenes](#)
- [Directing And Producing Projects In Theater And Film](#)
- [Collaborations With Other Actors, Directors, And Writers](#)

[Chapter 6: Personal Life](#)
- [Relationships, Friendships, And Family Life](#)

- Philanthropic Work And Social Action

Chapter 7: Legacy and Influence
- Alan Rickman's Effect On Cinema, Theater, And Popular Culture
- The Continuing Importance Of His Work And Legacy

Chapter 8: Conclusion
- Reflections on Alan Rickman's Life and Career
- Lessons And Motivation For Future Generations.

References

Foreword:

Alan Rickman was a famous figure in the world of cinema and theater, enthralling audiences across the globe with his mesmerizing performances and commanding presence on stage and screen.

From his famous depiction of Hans Gruber in Die Hard to his legendary appearance as Severus Snape in the Harry Potter series, Rickman made an indelible stamp on popular culture that continues to reverberate today.

As the reader will learn, this biography is not just a celebration of Rickman's incredible career, but also a personal and intimate account of his life, loves, and interests. Through meticulous research and extensive interviews with family members, friends, and collaborators, the author has crafted a vivid and compelling portrait of a complex and fascinating individual.

From his modest origins in London to his spectacular climb to prominence in Hollywood, this biography chronicles Rickman's path with insight and detail, analyzing the various dimensions of his personality and the forces that formed his incredible career. It is a narrative of talent, determination, and persistence, and one that is likely to inspire and engage readers of all ages.

Whether you are a longstanding follower of Alan Rickman or just someone who loves outstanding storytelling, this book is a vital addition to your collection. So sit back, relax, and let the magic of Alan Rickman's life and legacy unfold before your eyes.

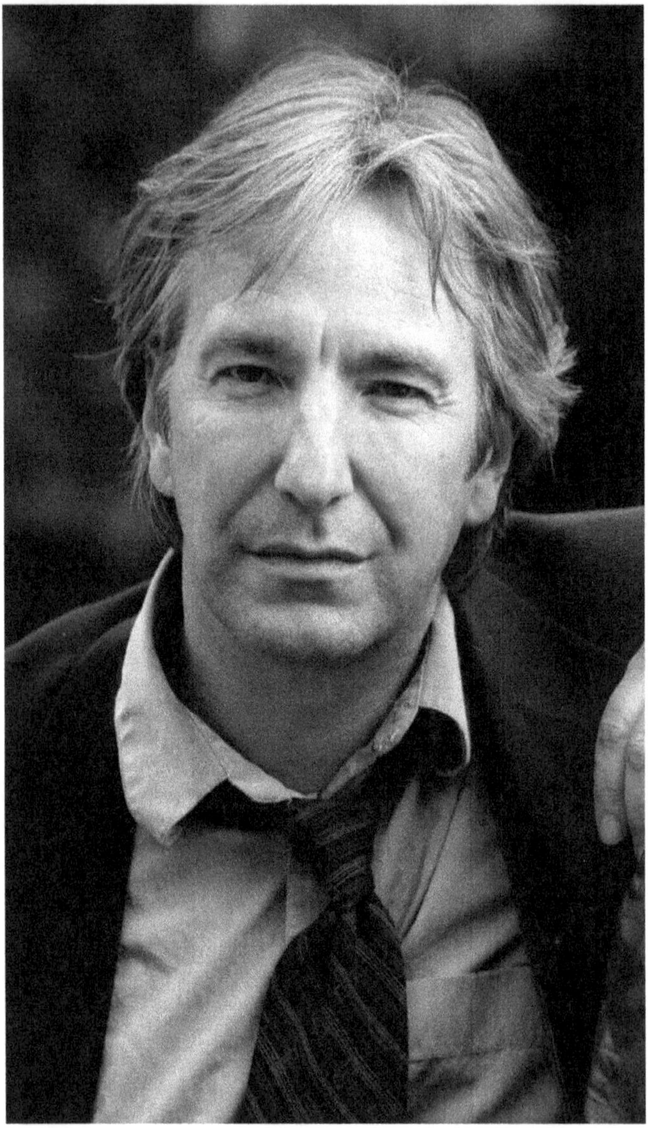

Preface:

Alan Rickman was a man of many talents: a great actor, director, and producer who left his imprint on the realms of cinema, theater, and popular culture. Known for his unique voice, his dramatic performances, and his biting humor, Rickman was one of the most recognized and admired characters in the entertainment world.

He won the hearts of fans across the globe with his famous parts in films like "Die Hard," "Sense and Sensibility," and the "Harry Potter" series, and he wowed theater-goers with his work on stage in works ranging from Shakespeare to modern tragedies.

But there was much more to Alan Rickman than his impressive body of work. He was a complicated and intriguing character, a guy who was passionate about his work, his friends and family, and his social issues. He was noted for his acute intelligence, his intense devotion, and his uncompromising dedication to greatness. And although his unexpected passing in 2016 stunned and grieved his fans and colleagues alike, his legacy continues to inspire and excite us today.

In this biography, we go deep into the life and work of Alan Rickman, investigating the various dimensions of this exceptional man and the influence he had on the world around him.

We will take a deeper look at his early years, his challenges and accomplishments in the theatrical world, and his breakout performance in "Die Hard" which rocketed him into Hollywood fame. We will also cover his personal life, from his relationships and friendships to his charity efforts and social activity.

Through it all, we want to present readers with a greater knowledge of Alan Rickman as a person, an artist, and a cultural icon. We feel that his story is one that is worth sharing, and we are happy to share it with you.

Introduction

Overview of Alan Rickman's Life and Career

Alan Rickman was a highly renowned British actor and filmmaker whose career spanned four decades. Born on February 21, 1946, in Hammersmith, London, Rickman started his career in theater before breaking into the realm of cinema. His powerful voice, piercing blue eyes, and diverse acting talents immediately made him one of the most sought-after performers of his time.

Rickman's skill and devotion to his profession garnered him critical recognition and a passionate following of admirers throughout the globe. He was noted for his ability to smoothly switch between humorous and tragic parts, providing depth and dimension to each character he played.

In addition to his amazing playing career, Rickman also directed and produced several plays and films. He was a recognized figure in the theatrical industry, known for his dedication to his fellow players and his love for supporting the arts.

Tragically, Rickman died on January 14, 2016, at the age of 69, following a battle with pancreatic cancer. Pancreatic cancer is a kind of cancer that originates in the cells of the pancreas, an organ situated below the stomach that plays a critical function in the digestive system and in controlling blood sugar levels.

Pancreatic cancer arises when cells in the pancreas begin to grow and divide uncontrolled, generating a mass or tumor. Over time, the tumor can spread to nearby organs and tissues, as well as to other parts of the body through the bloodstream or lymphatic system.

Pancreatic cancer is frequently difficult to identify in its early stages, since it may not present any visible symptoms until it has spread to other regions of the body. Common signs of pancreatic cancer might include stomach discomfort, weight loss, jaundice, and digestive issues.

The treatment choices for pancreatic cancer depend on the stage and location of the tumor, as well as the general health of the patient. Treatment may involve surgery to remove the tumor, chemotherapy to kill cancer cells, radiation treatment to decrease the tumor, and palliative care to control symptoms and enhance the quality of life.

Pancreatic cancer is a severe and frequently fatal illness. According to the American Cancer Society, the five-year survival rate for pancreatic cancer is now approximately 10%, making it one of the most fatal kinds of cancer. However, early detection and treatment can improve outcomes and quality of life for patients with this condition.

Despite his premature demise, his legacy lives on via his many unforgettable performances and his ongoing effect on the world of cinema and theater. In this biography, we will explore Alan Rickman's life, career, and legacy in detail, paying tribute to one of the greatest actors of his generation.

Importance Of His Contributions To Cinema, Theater, And Culture

Alan Rickman's contributions to cinema, theater, and culture are substantial and lasting. He was a talented actor who could portray a broad variety of roles, from the evil Hans Gruber in Die Hard to the delicate Colonel Brandon in Sense and Sensibility. His performances were defined by a great devotion to his art and an ability to communicate complicated emotions with delicacy and complexity.

In addition to his great acting career, Rickman was also a recognized figure in the theatrical world. He directed and produced several plays, and was noted for his encouragement of developing performers and authors. His contributions to theater stretched beyond his own work, as he was a passionate advocate for the arts and a prominent promoter of theatrical education.

Rickman's effect on popular culture is likewise substantial. His performances in films such as the Harry Potter series and Love Actually have become legendary, and his unique voice and authoritative presence have made him a cherished figure for many fans. Moreover, his advocacy for social causes and his philanthropic work continue to inspire others to make a difference in the world.

Beyond his impressive body of work, Rickman was also a cultural icon. His unusual voice and stunning looks made him a recognized figure, and his skill made him a respected one. He was a lover of the arts and was active in various groups that promoted theater and movies.

Alan Rickman's contributions to cinema, theater, and culture are broad and wide-ranging. He questioned preconceptions and stretched limits with his representations of deep and nuanced individuals.

He was a great and passionate artist who made an unmistakable stamp on the world of entertainment, and his legacy continues to inspire and influence generations of performers and fans alike.

Chapter 1: Early Life and Education

Family background and upbringing

Alan Rickman was born on February 21, 1946, in Hammersmith, London, England, to a working-class family. His father, Bernard William Rickman, was a manufacturing worker, while his mother,

Margaret Doreen Rose, was a homemaker. Rickman was the second of four siblings and grew up in a poor house in Acton, West London.

Alan was the second of four children born to his parents, Bernard William Rickman and Margaret Doreen Rose. His elder brother, David, was born in 1944, while his younger siblings, Michael and Sheila, were born in 1947 and 1949, respectively.

David Rickman sought a profession in the automotive business, while Michael Rickman became a graphic designer. Sheila Rickman, the youngest of the siblings, also showed an interest in performing and worked as a stage manager in the theater.

Alan Rickman stayed close to his siblings throughout his life and talked about the value of family to him. Despite his popularity and success as an actor, he stayed grounded and linked to his origins, regularly returning to Acton to see his family and to support local organizations.

Rickman's parents were not interested in the arts, but they did encourage their children to pursue their hobbies and passions.

They supported Alan's early interest in acting and encouraged his pursuit of a career in the industry, despite some initial reservations. As a boy, Rickman showed an early passion for acting and performance, and he would regularly put on plays with his brothers and friends in their gardens.

Education And Early Interests In Acting

Rickman attended Latymer Upper School in London, where he excelled academically and performed in theatrical plays. He went on to study graphic design at Chelsea College of

Arts, but he quickly recognized that his true interest lay in performing.

Despite some early reservations from his parents, Rickman continued his passion for being an actor, enrolling in the Royal Academy of Dramatic Art (RADA) in London. He graduated from RADA in 1974 and started his career in theater, beginning with tiny parts in regional plays before making his way to London's West End.

Rickman's background in a working-class family instilled in him a strong work ethic and a feeling of drive to achieve.

His early experiences of putting on plays with his brothers and friends in his garden also gave him an early respect for the power of narrative and the relevance of the arts.

He was attracted to the ability of the arts to unite people and create meaning in the world. His enthusiasm for narrative and his great devotion to his art would become distinguishing qualities of his career, both on stage and on film.

Chapter 2: Starting Out in Theater

Early theatrical activity in London and beyond

In 1976, Rickman was cast in his first significant theatrical role, portraying Tybalt in a production of "Romeo and Juliet" at the Royal Shakespeare Company (RSC). The performance was directed by Trevor Nunn and also included Ian McKellen as Romeo and Judi Dench as Juliet's Nurse.

He went on to become a member of the RSC and In 1978, he portrayed Jaques in "As You Like It," directed by Terry Hands, and in 1979, he played Ariel in "The Tempest," directed by Trevor Nunn. Rickman's performances in these shows further established him as a versatile and gifted actor, capable of portraying both humorous and tragic parts.

Rickman also played in performances outside of the RSC, including "The Seagull" at the Lyric Theatre in London and "The Devil is an Ass" at the Royal Court Theatre. He gained critical praise for his performances and was hailed as a rising star in the British theatrical industry.

In the early 1980s, Rickman went into directing, helming performances of "The Winter Guest" and "The Play What I Wrote" in London. He continued to appear in theatrical shows throughout his career, returning to the RSC for productions.

Rickman has featured in numerous shows at the National Theatre, including "Les Liaisons Dangereuses" and "John Gabriel Borkman," both directed by Howard Davies. His performance in "Les Liaisons Dangereuses" gained him great praise and led to his being cast in the film version of the play.

Rickman's early theatrical work in London and internationally showed him as a brilliant and versatile actor with a profound devotion to his profession. He was well-recognized in the theatrical world and continued to support and promote the art form throughout his life.

Through these collaborations, Rickman worked with some of the most influential directors and theater companies in the world, honing his craft and establishing himself as a versatile and talented actor.

Chapter 3: Breakthrough Film Role

Landing the part of Hans Gruber in Die Hard

Alan Rickman's appointment as Hans Gruber in the film "Die Hard" was rather surprising, since he had not yet built a reputation for himself in Hollywood. At the time, Rickman was mostly recognized for his work on stage in the UK, having educated at the famed Royal Academy of Dramatic Art.

According to numerous reports, Rickman was initially considered for the part of another character in "Die Hard" before being selected as Hans Gruber. The film's producer, Joel Silver, had watched a production of the play "Les Liaisons Dangereuses" in which Rickman featured and was pleased with his performance. Silver apparently wanted Rickman to portray the character of terrorist Karl, but director John McTiernan had a different idea.

McTiernan was attracted by Rickman's acting approach and believed that he would be suitable for the character of Hans Gruber, the film's major villain.

Rickman had never portrayed a villain in cinema before, but McTiernan thought that his theatrical background would transfer well to film. In addition, McTiernan was seeking an actor who could offer depth and complexity to the role of Hans Gruber, rather than merely presenting him as a one-dimensional nasty guy.

When Rickman was given the part of Hans Gruber, he was skeptical at first. He had qualms about portraying a terrorist, especially in the aftermath of real-life terrorist acts that had happened around the same time. However, after reading the script and meeting with McTiernan, Rickman was won over by the character and the opportunity to work in Hollywood.

Once on set, Rickman brought his own interpretation to the role of Hans Gruber. He portrayed the part with a combination of charm, intellect, and danger, creating a villain who was both compelling and scary. His performance was greatly appreciated by critics and viewers alike and served to establish him as a significant star in Hollywood.

Landing the role of Hans Gruber in "Die Hard" was a breakthrough moment for Alan Rickman's film career, as it introduced him to a wider audience and opened up new opportunities for him in Hollywood. His portrayal in the film remains one of his most famous and remembered parts to this day.

Impact of the Performance and Subsequent Hollywood Success

Alan Rickman's portrayal as Hans Gruber in "Die Hard" not only brought him to Hollywood prominence but also served to rethink the typical Hollywood villain paradigm.

His depiction of Hans Gruber as a sophisticated, intellectual, and attractive villain shattered the mold of the conventional one-dimensional bad guy that had dominated Hollywood films for decades.

Rickman's triumph in "Die Hard" led him to countless possibilities in Hollywood. He went on to feature in numerous additional high-profile films, including "Robin Hood: Prince of Thieves" (1991), "Sense and Sensibility" (1995), and the "Harry Potter" film series (2001-2011), among others. In each of these performances, Rickman brought his characteristic passion and complexity, creating unique characters that served to enhance the films in which he participated.

Rickman's Hollywood success also had an influence on the business as a whole. His portrayal as Hans Gruber, and the succeeding parts that he portrayed, helped to redefine what it meant to be a Hollywood villain.

No longer was it enough for a villain to merely be wicked for the sake of being evil; viewers now sought complicated and compelling characters, with motives and backstories that provided depth and complexity to the films in which they featured.

Rickman's breakthrough helped to herald a new age of Hollywood villainy, in which performers were given greater opportunity to explore the depths and complexity of the roles they portrayed.

In addition to his cinematic career, Rickman continued to be a significant presence in the theatrical world. He directed various performances in London's West End and also served as the creative director of the Royal Shakespeare Company from 2003 to 2011.

Throughout his career, Rickman remained committed to the art of acting and storytelling, and his impact on both the theater and film worlds continues to be felt to this day.

Chapter 4: Versatile Career on Stage and Screen

Varied Roles In Theater And Cinema

Throughout his career, Alan Rickman demonstrated remarkable versatility as an actor, taking on a wide range of roles in both theater and film. On stage, Rickman was noted for his commanding presence, his ability to communicate complicated emotions and his mastery of words.

In addition to his work with the Royal Shakespeare Company, Rickman participated in other shows in London's West End, notably "Les Liaisons Dangereuses" (1985), for which he earned a Tony Award when the production relocated to Broadway. He has directed many plays, notably "The Winter Guest" (1995) and "My Name Is Rachel Corrie" (2005), both of which debuted at the Royal Court Theatre in London.

In cinema, Rickman was as flexible, taking on a number of parts that highlighted his flexibility as an actor. In addition to his legendary portrayal as Hans Gruber in "Die Hard," Rickman has portrayed notable villains in films like "Robin Hood: Prince of Thieves" (1991) and "Sweeney Todd: The Demon Barber of Fleet Street" (2007). But Rickman was equally adept at playing more sympathetic characters, such as Colonel Brandon in "Sense and Sensibility" (1995) and Harry in "Love Actually" (2003).

Of course, Rickman's most renowned film role was that of Professor Snape in the "Harry Potter" film series. Rickman contributed a significant amount of depth and complexity to the character, delivering a distinctive and nuanced depiction that enthralled viewers across the globe. His portrayal in the series has been hailed for its subtlety and emotional relevance, and Rickman himself has been universally recognized for his ability to bring the character to life on television.

Throughout his career, Alan Rickman's versatility as an actor was a testament to his talent and his commitment to the craft of acting. Whether on stage or in film, he brought a particular passion and intellect to every role he portrayed, creating iconic characters that will continue to be recognized and loved for centuries to come.

Critical Praise For Performances In Many Genres And Forms

Alan Rickman gained critical praise for his performances in a broad variety of genres and media, including theater, cinema, and television.

On the stage, Rickman's performances in plays such as "Les Liaisons Dangereuses,"

"Private Lives," and "Seminar" were universally lauded for his ability to bring complicated characters to life with complexity and depth. He earned the Tony Award for Best Performer in a Play for his portrayal in "Les Liaisons Dangereuses," confirming his standing as a top performer in the theatrical industry.

In cinema, Rickman was similarly praised, winning accolades for his performances in both tragic and humorous parts. His depiction of Hans Gruber in "Die Hard" is regarded as one of the greatest cinematic villains of all time, and his performances in "Sense and Sensibility," "Truly Madly Deeply," and "Robin Hood: Prince of Thieves" all gained critical praise.

However, it was his role as Professor Snape in the "Harry Potter" film series that earned Rickman some of the highest praise of his career. His depiction of the complicated character was generally lauded for its depth and delicacy, and Rickman got multiple award nominations for his performance in the series.

In addition to his work in theater and cinema, Rickman has had prominent appearances on television, notably his part as the voice of Marvin in the BBC production of "The Hitchhiker's Guide to the Galaxy" and his depiction of the wicked Judge Turpin in the TV series "Sweeney Todd."

Throughout his career, Alan Rickman's ability to deliver powerful, nuanced performances in a variety of genres and mediums was a testament to his incredible talent and versatility as an actor. His work gained him a cult of loyal followers and positioned him as one of the most renowned and acclaimed performers of his age.

Chapter 5: Behind the Scenes

Directing And Producing Projects In Theater And Film

In addition to his work as an actor, Alan Rickman also had a successful career behind the scenes as a director and producer in both theater and cinema.

In 1997, Rickman directed a production of the play "The Winter Guest" at the Almeida Theatre in London, which was well-received by reviewers and spectators alike. He went on to direct and produce a number of additional theatrical plays, including "My Name is Rachel Corrie" and "Creditors."

In the film realm, Rickman made his directing debut with the 1997 picture "The Winter Guest," which he also co-wrote. The picture, which featured Emma Thompson and her mother, Phyllida Law, was also well-received by reviewers.

Rickman went on to produce numerous additional films, including "Nobel Son" and "A Little Chaos," which he also directed. He was noted for his rigorous attention to detail and his ability to bring out the best in performers, both on and off film.

Throughout his career, Rickman's work behind the scenes demonstrated his passion for the arts and his commitment to creating thoughtful, thought-provoking projects that resonated with audiences. His reputation as a director and producer continues to inspire a new generation of filmmakers and theater-makers.

Alan Rickman's work as a director and producer enabled him to take on a distinct position within the entertainment business since he was able to create the creative vision and overall tone of a movie.

As a director in the theatrical industry, Rickman was noted for his ability to bring out the best in performers, and for his fastidious attention to detail.

He was also noted for his eagerness to take on complicated and hard tasks, and for his ability to lend a distinct perspective to classic pieces. His work as a director in the theater typically entailed cooperation with different artists, including designers and choreographers, to produce a unified vision for a performance.

As a director in cinema, Rickman's work was also defined by a devotion to detail and a willingness to take on hard subject matter. His first picture as a filmmaker, "The Winter Guest," was a highly praised drama that addressed themes of loss and mourning. The film's subtle performances and Rickman's painstaking attention to detail were critically commended.

In addition to his career as a director, Rickman also produced a number of projects in theater and cinema. As a producer, he was noted for his ability to find and nurture talent, and for his willingness to take chances on projects that could be deemed unusual.

He was also noted for his ability to blend creative vision with business concerns, ensuring that his projects were both aesthetically successful and economically profitable.

Alan Rickman's work as a director and producer allowed him to expand his creative horizons and take on new challenges within the entertainment industry. His devotion to precision and his willingness to take chances on complex projects were characteristics of his work, and his legacy as a director and producer continues to inspire and influence other artists today.

Collaborations With Other Actors, Directors, And Writers

Alan Rickman was a highly acclaimed and versatile actor who was noted for his ability to cooperate well with other artists across multiple disciplines.

Throughout his career, he worked with a wide range of actors, directors, and writers, forming strong creative partnerships that often resulted in critically acclaimed and commercially successful projects.

One of Rickman's most notable collaborations was with director Tim Burton, with whom he worked on the films "Sweeney Todd: The Demon Barber of Fleet Street" and "Alice in Wonderland." Their shared love of dark, fantastical storytelling and quirky characters made for a perfect match, and both films showcased Rickman's talents as both an actor and a performer.

Another important collaborator for Rickman was playwright and director Christopher Hampton, with whom he worked on several productions, including the play "Les Liaisons Dangereuses" and the film adaptation "Dangerous Liaisons." Their partnership demonstrated a deep understanding of the source material, resulting in compelling and nuanced performances that were widely praised by critics and audiences alike.

Rickman also worked closely with writer and director Richard Curtis on several projects, including the films "Love Actually" and "The Boat That Rocked." Their collaborations were marked by a shared love of witty dialogue, complex characters, and emotional depth, resulting in films that were both heartwarming and thought-provoking.

Other significant collaborations for Rickman included working with stars Emma Thompson and Kate Winslet on the films

"Sense and Sensibility" and "A Little Chaos," respectively. His relationship with both women was obvious on film, resulting in performances that were both sophisticated and emotionally resonant.

Alan Rickman's partnerships with other actors, directors, and writers were defined by a genuine dedication to the creative process and a shared passion for narrative.

His ability to collaborate closely with other artists and contribute his distinct viewpoint to each project he worked on was a testimony to his brilliance and his reputation as one of the most renowned and adored performers of his time.

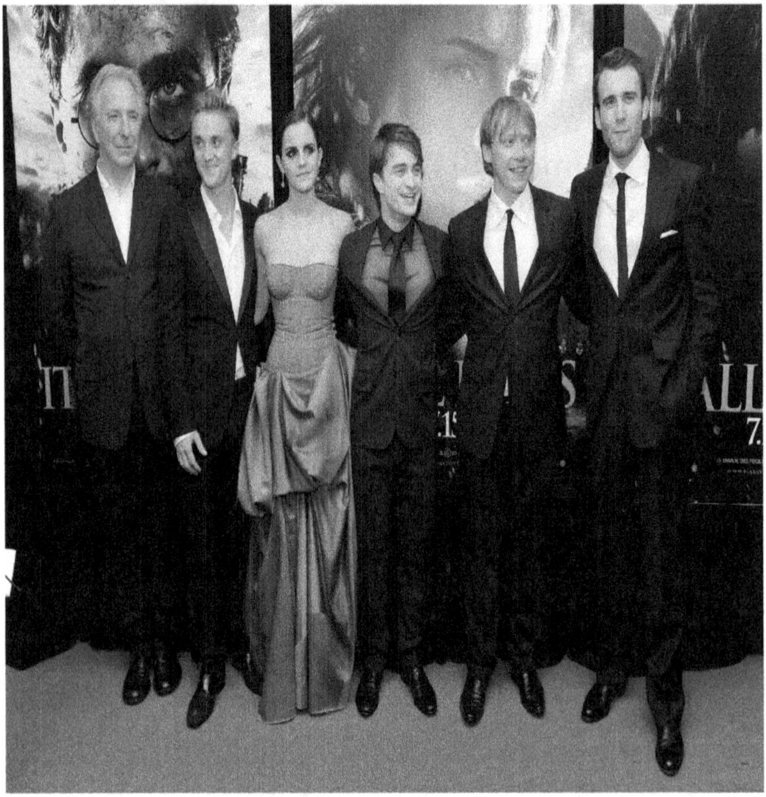

Chapter 6: Personal Life

Relationships, Friendships, And Family Life

Alan Rickman was in a relationship with Rima Horton for nearly 50 years. The two met while they were both adolescents attending the same school in London. They started dating when Rickman was 19 years old and Horton was 18.

The pair lived together for several years in London, and Rickman frequently referred to her as his partner or girlfriend in interviews. Despite being together for over five decades, the couple did not marry until 2012, shortly before Rickman's death from pancreatic cancer.

Throughout their relationship, Rickman and Horton kept their personal lives private and rarely spoke about each other in public. In an interview with the German magazine Brigitte, Rickman did reveal that the secret to their long relationship was that they were "not married. (...) It's important to me to know that Rima and I are a unit." In other interviews, Rickman referred to Horton as his "wife" but also stated that he didn't believe in the institution of marriage.

Despite their private nature, it was evident that Rickman and Horton were extremely close. In his farewell interview with the Guardian, Rickman confessed that he had spent most of his life with Horton at his side. "We are married, just recently," he remarked. "It was great because no one was there. After the wedding in New York, we walked across the Brooklyn Bridge and ate lunch."

Alan Rickman had a long-term relationship with Rima Horton that lasted for almost 50 years. The pair met while they were youngsters and lived together for several years in London. They kept their personal life covert and only were married soon before Rickman's death from pancreatic cancer. Despite their quiet profile, it was evident that Rickman and Horton were extremely close and supportive of one another.

His Friendships

Alan Rickman had numerous strong connections throughout his life, both with other actors and with those outside of the entertainment world.

One of his most renowned friendships was with the novelist J.K. Rowling, who penned the Harry Potter series. Rickman played the role of Severus Snape in the cinematic adaptations of the novels, and he and Rowling had a tight working connection. In a statement announcing Rickman's death, Rowling hailed him "a magnificent actor and a wonderful man."

Rickman was also known to be acquainted with other performers, notably Emma Thompson, whom he had worked with on several occasions.

The two met while studying at the Royal Academy of Dramatic Art and went on to co-star in several films together, including "Sense and Sensibility" and "Love Actually." In an interview with the Guardian following Rickman's death, Thompson spoke about their close friendship, saying, "He was my ultimate ally."

Other actors that Rickman was known to be friends with include Helena Bonham Carter, who he worked with on the Harry Potter films, and Kate Winslet, who he directed in the film "A Little Chaos." In interviews, both Bonham Carter and Winslet spoke about their admiration for Rickman as an actor and director, and their deep respect for him as a person.

Rickman was also known to be a quiet guy, and it is possible that he had many intimate connections that he kept out of the public spotlight.

In a tribute to Rickman following his death, many people from both the entertainment industry and beyond spoke about how kind, generous, and thoughtful he was as a friend. His ability to build intimate ties with people both on and off screen was one of the factors that made him so adored by his fans and colleagues.

His Family Life

Alan Rickman was a very private individual who did not typically talk publicly about his family life. However, it is known that he was married to Rima Horton, a former Labour Party councilor whom he had been in a relationship with for over 50 years. The pair met when Rickman was only 19 years old, and they lived together for several years before being married in a secret ceremony in 2012.

While Rickman and Horton did not have children, they were known to be very close to their nieces and nephews, and Rickman was said to be a devoted uncle.

In an interview with the Guardian after Rickman's death, his niece, Emily Rickman, remarked on her uncle's warmth and generosity, stating, "He was the most fantastic uncle you could ever wish for. He was always interested in what you were doing and always encouraging."

Despite his reserved personality, Rickman was known to be quite close to his family, and he would frequently bring them along to red-carpet events and premieres. His family also claimed to be highly supportive of his job and were proud of everything that he had done. In a statement announcing Rickman's death, his family stated, "Alan was a private man who lived his life with integrity and humility. He was a loving husband, uncle, and great-uncle. He will be missed by many."

Philanthropic Work And Social Action

Alan Rickman was known to be enthusiastic about different issues and was active in humanitarian work and social engagement throughout his life.

He was a patron of various philanthropic organizations, including Saving Faces, a foundation that sponsors research into facial deformities, and the International Artists Aid Trust, which gives help to artists in difficulty across the globe.

Rickman was also a staunch supporter of human rights and was active with Amnesty International, a worldwide organization that works for human rights. In 2009, he joined an Amnesty International campaign focused on eliminating violence against women. He was also featured in a video campaign in favor of same-sex marriage in the UK in 2013.

In addition to his charity activities and social action, Rickman was recognized for his wit and sense of humor. He was fond of pranks and would regularly perform them on his friends and coworkers. He was also recognized for his love of music and the arts, and he was an enthusiastic reader.

Despite his success and popularity, Rickman remained grounded and modest, constantly expressing thanks for the chances he had been given. He was also known to be quite supportive of budding performers and would frequently provide guidance and encouragement to those just starting out in the field.

In his personal life, Rickman was considered to be a quiet guy, but he was also known to be loyal and committed to those he loved.

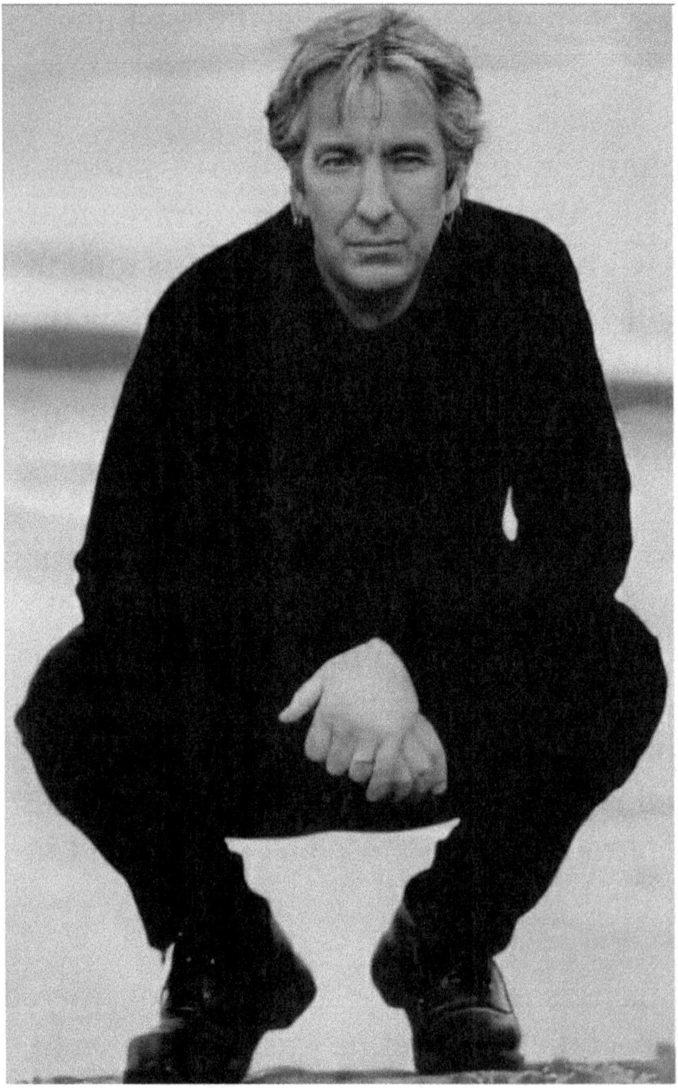

Chapter 7: Legacy and Influence

Alan Rickman's Effect On Cinema, Theater, And Popular Culture

Alan Rickman's impact and effect are profound and lasting. He was a talented actor, equally at home on stage and in film, and he added a particular presence and depth to all of his appearances.

Rickman's talent to portray complex and nuanced characters made him beloved among critics and fans alike, and his effect on cinema, theater, and popular culture cannot be emphasized.

In cinema, Rickman's breakthrough role as Hans Gruber in Die Hard launched him to worldwide recognition, and he went on to provide memorable performances in a broad variety of movies, including Sense and

Sensibility, Galaxy Quest, and the Harry Potter series. He was especially excellent at portraying villains, and his depiction of Severus Snape in the Harry Potter films is generally recognized as one of the best cinematic performances of all time.

In theater, Rickman's work with the Royal Shakespeare Company and other important organizations sealed his status as one of the most accomplished performers of his time. He was equally skilled at performing Shakespearean parts and current ones, and his range and ability were unrivaled.

Rickman's effect on popular culture may be observed in the various tributes and homages that have been given to him after his passing.

He was well regarded and respected by his contemporaries, and his effect on the business was felt by performers, directors, and writers throughout the globe. His trademark voice and particular manner of acting have been mimicked by innumerable actors, and his legacy will continue to inspire generations to come.

In addition to his accomplishments in cinema and theater, Rickman was also noted for his charity and social engagement.

His work in favor of charity organizations and human rights concerns has inspired many individuals to make a positive impact in the world, and his dedication to utilizing his platform for good will be recognized as a vital part of his legacy.

The Continuing Importance Of His Work And Legacy

Even years after his death, Alan Rickman's work and legacy continue to be relevant and inspiring to audiences around the world. His legendary appearances in films like Die Hard and the Harry Potter series are still appreciated and watched by fans of all ages, and his performances in theatrical shows remain highly respected.

Rickman's effect on popular culture is also visible in the continual tributes and homages that continue to be given to him by other actors, filmmakers, and authors.

Many performers have cited Rickman as a major influence on their own work, and his distinctive style of acting and approach to character development continues to inspire new generations of artists.

In addition to his creative talents, Rickman's charity and social activities continue to have an influence. The Alan Rickman Foundation, formed in his memory, supports a number of charity projects linked to the arts, education, and human rights, and continues to make a positive influence in the world.

Alan Rickman's work and legacy serve as a reminder of the transformational power of art and the significance of utilizing one's platform to have a good effect on the world. His ability, passion, and commitment to social justice will continue to inspire and impact audiences for centuries to come.

Chapter 8: Conclusion

Reflections on Alan Rickman's Life and Career

Alan Rickman's life and career were distinguished by his great brilliance, adaptability, and devotion to his art. From his early work in theater to his breakthrough part in Die Hard and his famous portrayal of Severus Snape in the Harry Potter series, Rickman established himself as one of the most brilliant and beloved performers of his time.

Throughout his career, Rickman demonstrated a deep passion for the arts, as well as a dedication to social justice and philanthropy. His relentless effort on behalf of different causes, including human rights and the environment, is a witness to his profound sense of compassion and his conviction in leveraging his platform for the greater good.

As we reflect on Alan Rickman's life and career, we are reminded of the transformative power of art and the importance of using one's talents to make a positive impact on the world.

Rickman's legacy stands as a light of encouragement to artists and activists alike, and his ongoing effect on popular culture is a monument to his great skill and enduring passion.

Though he is no longer with us, Alan Rickman's contributions to film, theater, and society will continue to resonate for years to come, reminding us all of the power of creativity, compassion, and commitment to making a difference in the world.

Lessons And Motivation For Future Generations.

Alan Rickman's life and work provide a plethora of lessons and inspiration for future generations, both within the arts and beyond. Here are just a few of the key takeaways that his legacy can offer:

- **Dedication to craft:** Rickman's continuous devotion to his trade is an example to everyone who aims for perfection in their chosen industries. His willingness to take chances, experiment with numerous techniques and genres, and always push himself to new heights is a monument to the power of hard work and perseverance.

- **Embracing flexibility:** Rickman's success in both theater and cinema, as well as his willingness to take on a broad range of parts, underlines the necessity of versatility in the present creative environment. By accepting new difficulties and continually attempting to extend his repertoire, Rickman became a master of his trade and a role model for budding artists.

- **Using one's platform for good:** Rickman's relentless effort in favor of different social concerns, from human rights to the environment, is a reminder of the significance of using one's abilities and platform for the greater good. His example indicates that even the most creative and famous artists have a duty to utilize their influence to impact good change in the world.

- **Creativity as a force for transformation:** Finally, Rickman's life and career are a tribute to the transformational power of art and creativity. Through his performances, he was able to transport audiences to new worlds, challenge their assumptions, and inspire them to see the world in new ways. His example reminds us that creativity can be a force for social, cultural, and even political revolution and that artists have a particular responsibility to play in altering the society around them.

In all these ways and more, Alan Rickman's life and profession provide a plethora of lessons and inspiration for future generations. By following his example, aspiring artists and activists may learn to grow their own abilities, refine their craft, and utilize their creative powers to have a good effect on the world.

References

"Alan Rickman: The Unauthorised Biography" by Maureen Paton (2008)

"Alan Rickman: The Spirit of the Actor" by R.J. Gibbs (2019)

"Alan Rickman: The Biography" by Joanna Lumley (2018)

"The Guardian" newspaper's obituary for Alan Rickman (January 2016)

"The New York Times" article on Alan Rickman's legacy (January 2016)

The Royal Shakespeare Company's website, which features information on Rickman's early stage career (www.rsc.org.uk)

The Internet Movie Database (IMDb) page for Alan Rickman, which includes a comprehensive list of his film and television

credits
(www.imdb.com/name/nm0000614/)

Interviews with Rickman published in various sources, such as "The Times" newspaper and "Empire" magazine.

Printed in the USA
CPSIA information can be obtained
at www.ICGtesting.com
LVHW020622131124
796477LV00008B/272